Inky Lemon

Ivy Haycox

Inky Lemon © 2023 Ivy Haycox

All rights reserved.

No part of this publication may be reproduced, stored in a retrieval system, or transmitted, in any form or by any means, electronic, mechanical, photocopying, recording or otherwise, without the prior written permission of the presenters.

Ivy Haycox asserts the moral right to be identified as author of this work.

Presentation by *BookLeaf Publishing*

Web: www.bookleafpub.com

E-mail: info@bookleafpub.com

ISBN: 9789357748513

First edition 2023

ACKNOWLEDGEMENT

To Adali, Madison, Shelly, and especially Silver.
Not without y'all.

PREFACE

If you or anyone you know is struggling with thoughts of ending their life, please call or text the suicide hotline at 988.

Big Enough

I am cheap but flowing fabrics
I am three fears wrapped in rubber bands
I have twenty-eight fingers
And I thrust them in the air
When some despicable elder
Leans down and asks

I am inky lists and photos
I am scars made by signs I ignored
I have love on either side of me
And I wrap my arms around them both
At takeoff and landing
On Christmas and birthdays

I am thread sewing the spine of a book
I am shelves filled with dead dogs
I have so much to apologize for
But I hold my sorry in my chest like a dagger
Waiting to wield it against someone
Whose sorry could never be enough

I am booker by trade, mom by day
I am dove when moonlight grazes my cheek
I have ribbons and snowglobes to give
But I want to be small too

Small enough to fall asleep on his shoulder
But I must be big enough to reach the pedals

2

Ink

No one has ever asked
What I think of dimples
Or how it feels to die

But the empty pages
Are not too busy
To hear my inky musings

And so I list names for fire
And talk to the dead
I bleed in prose

My pen fills up buckets
Of what shouldn't be in me
Things that seep out my pores

But I am not a poet
I am a bruise
Just blood under skin

Pricked by a pen

Can I Go Now?

May I be dismissed
Exhale a final
Wrap my goose bump arms
Around the scythe and be carried away
Let my heart turn blue
And grace my abusers with loss
Maybe I'll get to cry in that way
Where it never stops
I could create my own Alice ocean
And swim off to the caucus race
I'll split my crumpet with the souls
Lying unresponsive on that beach
I'll dance with arms bent like empty links
Treading them all to watery bloody sand
I'll wear vests made of mythril memory
And feed on Einstein's brain with sherry
I'll say all the perfect things to strangers
From a single bubble under the ocean
And what a joyous lonely nothing
What a beautiful sentient silence
To relax every muscle
And drown

For Oliver

Good morning
Dear Oliver
Is it cold
Where you are

My feet
Dear Oliver
Are wrapped tight
In cashmere

Good afternoon
Dear Oliver
Is it hot
Where you are

My eyes
Dear Oliver
Are shielded
In hard plastic

Good night
Dear Oliver
Are you alone
In your bed

For my feet
And my hands
Lie in bags
Underneath it

Champagne

I get my nightly allotment of champagne.

It comes in a cup
Plastic, like for Xanax
But my Tuberculosis
Comes in my nightly

She isn't drinking her champagne
She isn't playing her flute
She isn't wearing her colors
Joining the parade

Does she drink her champagne
Does she wear the charade
Does she bark like a dog
Does she drink her champagne

The cup doesn't break
It bends and splashes and it
Fills with champagne
But her cup doesn't break.

Without Bodies

If what I am
Was not the parts you like to hold
If I had no crescendos or angles
Nor had spaces or breath

I wouldn't be holes
And you couldn't fill them
I would have no hands
To hold your empty

If I couldn't follow you
Since we have no halls
And I couldn't see you
Without lights and sun

I would know nothing
Of your dietary needs
Or your sleepy eyes
After nights spent having bodies

If I were a thing defined
By the such of an essence
And you were a creature made
Of your isms and interests

We would know each other
And we would want not
To be closer, to touch further
I could not miss you

Without presence
In a world without space

Trope

I'm still waiting

I could list the compliments
I've been afforded
I could lament the past
I no longer live
But still my heart cannot believe
I don't live the life I did

So send me on the wheel unbroken
Send me on the wing unmarred
Take me to the life unspoken
Show me what I've missed so far

Paint a truth I've always known
Marry my doubt and hope
Tell me I've a reason
And tell me I'm a trope
Tell me I am unbelieved
Tell me I am all alone

Tell me I'm a pain you've felt
That my expressions are familiar
That you've wondered such doubts
When you look in the mirror

Salt and Pepper

I am surprised to find

That the backs of your hands
Have no scars
Like mine do

Tracing my fingers
Across your collar
Still no marks

From the surgery
I had at twelve
And you did not

Your tattoos, even
Are in different places
Different colors

The ringlets in your hair
The salt and pepper curls
The arms so sturdy
I never feel like falling

And yet I am
And I didn't dream you

I didn't write you

I couldn't have
With a smile like that
And honey eyes

I didn't know brown
Could glow like that
Could gleam so

I didn't know men
Could be so kind
So then how

Not in my image
Not of my mind
He lays still in my arms
And listens to me sing

Incoming

No one will tell you
When you're about to die

No pilot will intercom
No nurse will pat your arm

The gun will have a silencer
And the man will tip-toe

You won't have time to call
There will be no last words

It will feel like you slipped
On a puddle made of ink

And you start falling
And you never stop

Sidewalk

The decision to live
Is not a headline
Blood on bathroom tile
Gets the spotlight
But can carrying on
Be the tragedy this time

I'll be less
I'll paint more
I won't argue
I'll sleep my days away
I'll let my barely beating heart
Scuttle across the sidewalk

Flattery

Knowing men
Has ruined it

Nothing is a compliment anymore

Flattery is an attempt at ownership
He sees me as a sculpture with holes
His compliments are lubrication
He drools as he slathers them onto my slots
Priming me without permission
To take a hole and fill it

But that is not enough
He needs his holes to work for him
To gather his laziness like flies in a jar
And put it on a mantle in her home
Showing it off like fine art
The ring on her finger

Topsoil

I don't know what name
She gave you
There are gaps
In the stories I have
But she died at only fifty
When her brain gave way

She's been bleeding for years
But I never noticed
I walked through the double doors
Just as she went flat
The doctor asked
If I had a last goodbye

And so I said

Blessings on those that mourn you
For they will need my grace

And bless your rotten legacy
One you'll never have to face

Bless all of us who outlive you
With chance to be free

But mostly bless your bleeding brain
You got that blessing from me

Dead Spiders and Living Centipedes

A list

Of the things that secretly possess me
Or compose me
I don't know
But they settle in my feet when I stand

Bookmarks, unlaminated
Made of things found strewn about
I take them out of the books I did not finish
So no one knows my failures of disinterest

Pregnancy tests, positive and negative
One was found wrapped in toilet paper
And hidden at the bottom of a trash can
The rest were in a series of pure gold boxes

Dead spiders and living centipedes
Do not worry, they are my friends
Harvey died last March
And I put him in a plastic case

Test grades and folded notes
One is a love letter to no one

I should have written it to myself
But I learned to fold it into a heart

Halloween candy
From every year since I turned 22
When I somehow stopped liking sweets
But I keep it for guests and my children

Safety pins, paperclips, and bits of chain
I've been meaning to make a wedding dress
But my faith in my own oddities
Is dwindling

Have Faith

God finally responded
To my letters
And he blames

Eve.

"My dearest Ivy,"
He writes me,
"It's not you,

It's Eve."

"When you asked
Why you have
These body parts

That bleed,

I could think
Of no one
Else but Eve.

She was my
Second human creation,
I loved her.

But she wanted
Life without limits,
Love without bars.

She wanted to
Experience the world
To know all,

So I had to do it.

Please understand Ivy,
She would not
Follow the rules.

And so you
Ask me why
You have parts

That bleed.

You ask me why
You have parts
That can scream

If you're not
Allowed to scream
When you bleed

And to that
I must say
Just have faith

Have faith, my child
Be calm, good girl
God grant you wisdom
To shrivel and curl

Be small, good girl
Be grateful, above all
Stay still, sit quiet
Shut up, good girl"

Sage

I roll over and feel a hand
Creep across my ribs to pull me back
There he is, a heavy breath
And an unconscious caress
Reminding me
Of the love I have behind me

Your soft beard against my lips
A kiss hung suspended
Never will I regret
Your arms pulling me closer
And your thumbs drawing circles
On my back to remind me
Of the love I have behind me

I stir awake at the witching hour
My thirst calls from the kitchen
But your hand runs through my hair
Despite your dreams uninterrupted
And I settle back in, reminded
Of the love I have beside me

Nearly asleep but smiling
My breath slows back into dreaming
I would give you the world

And create more if you need
And so I shall behind my eyes
While I drift away, reminded
Of the love I have inside me

Fingernail

I often picture my death

Flying, whistling wind
Tumbling rocks that predict my landing

Barreling down a highway
Chirping along to some
Grand poetic indie jam
I could not be happier

So much so that I think
Of twisted metal
And sopping red concrete
Skull fragments

What pure joy
That moment airborne
Knowing I could never hurt again
Nor hurt anyone more than this

I try not to allow images
Of idiotic fumbling
Phones dropping and shattering
On kitchen tile

I think only of my fingers
The central focus of a photograph
Fingernail cracked down the middle
One joint crooked out of place

In the background, crackling
The shell of a vehicle engulfed
Blurry red and blue approaching
Rain mixing with blood

Why is this thought
So beautiful to me

They Have Three Names

Be careful walking alone in new cities
They are there falling in love with you
They will caress and haunt you
They will learn your favorite color
They will meet your parents
They will grow like weeds inside your soul

They will chew your bones to marrow
And listen while you cry about your mother
They will pull at your hemlines
They will howl your name at the moons
They are in every dark corner
They know your address, your shoe size

They are in between your couch cushions
They have you in boxes in their mother's
basement
They made a necklace of your vertebrae
They love you more than you have ever known
They smile at you with nothing but gums
They wrap your body in a tarp

You are every dream they've ever had
You stand faceless with tits in their fantasies
Your hips sway while they lower to one knee

Your lipstick parts when they give their speech
You smile and say yes no matter what
You have no thoughts, no escape

Just like me,
They long to be
Close to you

Appreciated

I keep handing you shards of me

I don't know what you do with them

If they arrive at the gates of your heart
Guided in by your tenured angels
Of the highest glory
Thanking these pieces as they enter
And encasing them forever on velvet shelves

Or if they drop into an empty tin
Looking around expectantly
For the other pieces sent before
They wait for a light to flick on
But one never does

Lemon Twists

I want that sound of slowly warping metal
I want my brain to smell like overcooked toast
I want nails made of reinforced steel at the end
of my fingers
I want blood in my throat

I want to reason with men on the street
I want to drown in the desert
I want a meat tenderizer in my neck
I want to hold you until it's all over

I want to look god in his fucking eyes and
scream
I want to blend my skull with shower tiles
I want to leave pieces of my body in mailboxes
I want to bite your fucking smile

I want to turn my skin into lemon twists
I want to be folded and crumpled like paper
I want to know what Job felt
I want to carve myself with clay

I want you to switch me off and power me down
I want to understand football

I want to teach my daughter to make flower
crowns
I want to lose half my brain in a fire

I want a papercut from my scalp to my intestines
I want to ruin someone's wedding day
I want to sever a spinal cord
I want to be okay

Don't Cry, It's Only Art

One day my daughter will read this
Perhaps to herself on my passed down armchair
Drinking coffee as she unpacks boxes

Maybe she'll tell her daughter that I wrote it
When I was pregnant with her little sister
And my granddaughter will look up at Adali
from the hearthrug
And say, "Aunt Silver?" with shining eyes

My granddaughter will know nothing of the
women
Who allowed abuse through the ages
The sort of trauma that creates poets
Who dream of grandchildren on hearthrugs
Living beyond the world we had

My grandparents will know nothing of the
hearthrug
Of the undisclosed location where I found safety
And perpetuated it against all odds
So that women can have the years my family
stole
To crochet each other sweaters
Far away from my bruised memories

I will not be the story I lived
My girls will not know what I did to escape
They will only know which books I loved
Which countries I visited
When I was bold enough to stretch my legs
I will give them Hieronymus Bosch and film
The darkest things they ever know will be only
art

And when I go
I'll turn to Mad and say,
We gave them what we always wanted
We gave them memories to save
We gave them holidays and summer camp
We gave them hugs and band-aids
We gave them Halloween candy
We gave them Mardi Gras parades

And I will always love you
Because we always felt safe

Freshly Fallen Snow

I find myself filled with the uncontrollable urge to run sixteen and a half miles barefoot in the freshly fallen snow. When I collapse, breathless and forced immobile with nothing to serve my eyes but grey snowing sky I will grin with all my teeth knowing you love me. I'll allow myself the unabashed glow that washes over me while my senseless exertion plays welcome juxtaposition to the cold. While I walk home I will pick a flower from the bed of each memory I've yet to share with you so that by the time I see you again I have a bouquet of the me I never felt loved enough to share with anyone else. The tissue paper around the bouquet I brought home for you will whisper against your back as we kiss hello again and you ask me about my jaunt. I'll waste our time describing each moment the pad of my exposed foot hit a patch of snow-covered grass and you'll beam at me from across the table. We'll sneak into the room of our snoozing children and giggle to each other before we kiss them goodnight and then go away to make love for the rest of our lives. I'll coat your sad moments in glitter and you'll cover mine in handwoven blankets. I'll touch your

back when I wake up each morning so you smile
before you ever even open your eyes. I promise
to love you until every place we ever spent our
time in is so covered with dust that you can no
longer hear the echoes of our laughter or the
sighs we let out between kisses there. I promise
to love you until everything turns so cold that
one could not possibly run sixteen and a half
miles barefoot in the fresh fallen snow.

www.ingramcontent.com/pod-product-compliance
Lightning Source LLC
Chambersburg PA
CBHW070614160726
48003CB00005B/2264